How to run a small development project

by a 'Geneva Group'

INTERMEDIATE TECHNOLOGY PUBLICATIONS 1986

Practical Action Publishing Ltd
27a Albert Street, Rugby, CV21 2SG, Warwickshire, UK
www.practicalactionpublishing.org

© Intermediate Technology Publications 1986

First published 1986\Digitised 2013

ISBN 10: 0 94668 847 8
ISBN 13: 9780946688470
ISBN Library Ebook: 9781780442457
Book DOI: http://dx.doi.org/10.3362/9781780442457

All rights reserved. No part of this publication may be reprinted or reproduced or utilized in any form or by any electronic, mechanical, or other means, now known or hereafter invented, including photocopying and recording, or in any information storage or retrieval system, without the written permission of the publishers.

A catalogue record for this book is available from the British Library.

The authors, contributors and/or editors have asserted their rights under the Copyright Designs and Patents Act 1988 to be identified as authors of their respective contributions.

Since 1974, Practical Action Publishing has published and disseminated books and information in support of international development work throughout the world. Practical Action Publishing is a trading name of Practical Action Publishing Ltd (Company Reg. No. 1159018), the wholly owned publishing company of Practical Action. Practical Action Publishing trades only in support of its parent charity objectives and any profits are covenanted back to Practical Action (Charity Reg. No. 247257, Group VAT Registration No. 880 9924 76).

CONTENTS

Preface   vii

PART I: STARTING AND CARRYING ON THE PROJECT

Chapter 1 Starting the project   1

A. Introduction   1

B. The aim of the project   1

C. Setting up the organization   2

D. People working in the project   2

E. Training   4

F. The timetable   4

G. Supplies needed   6

H. Money needed   7

Chapter 2 Running the project   13

A. Introduction   13

B. Keeping to the timetable   13

C. Money   14

D. The management of supplies   29

E. Managing the people working in the project   30

F. Relationships with partners   31

PART II WORKING WITH YOUR PARTNERS

	Page
Introduction	33
Chapter 1 The partner abroad explains who he is	35
Chapter 2 The project organizer puts his project to his partner	36
A. The nature of the project	37
B. The structure and organization of the project	37
C. People working in the project	37
D. The timetable of the project	37
E. Supplies and equipment	38
F. Training	38
Chapter 3 Dialogue between partners	39
A. Introduction	39
B. Duties of the partner abroad	39
C. Duties of the project organizers	40
D. Visits to the project	41

LIST OF ILLUSTRATIONS

1.	People needed for the ABC training project	3
2.	Example of a project timetable	5
3.	Supplies needed once and for all	6
4.	Supplies needed regularly	7
5.	Details of the costs of people working in the project	8
6.	Example of a budget	12

		Page
7.	Cash book of Project ABC	15
8.	Receipt for an advance	16
9.	Receipt for unspent money	16
10.	Receipt	17
11.	Receipt for a loan	18
12.	Loan agreement	19
13.	Monthly budget of a training centre	21
14.	Comparison of income and expenses	23
15.	Control of the monthly budget	24
16.	Cumulative expenditure and income month by month	26
17.	Record of millet stocks	29

PREFACE

This manual is intended to help the managers of small development projects in the Third World to design and manage their projects well. It tries, in particular, to help them to see future problems so that they can deal with them in good time.

Managing means looking after the people who are helping - as well as the money and materials. In some cases, Development projects in the Third World will need to obtain support from organizations in the North. Part of the manual deals with relations between partners in the South and the North.

There is an important difference between Parts I and II. The intention of the authors is to help those responsible for a small Development project in the Third World to be confident that their project is likely to go well. This should be possible if they can answer all the questions in Part I satisfactorily. If there are questions which they cannot answer properly, they should think more about them before proceeding. If, on the other hand, they have thought it through properly, their partners in the North should not subject them to additional questions.

Part II starts with the Northern partners introducing themselves (see page 35 - which the Northern partner should complete before distributing this manual). After the Introduction, Part II is intended simply to ensure that the partner can check that those responsible for the project in the South are proceeding effectively and are following Part I. Part II also aims to encourage open and trusting relations between the partners. Openness and trust are essential, but cannot be achieved by formal reports alone. The intention of Part II is to explain how to lighten the burden, while increasing the trust, in the relations between the partners.

This manual has been produced by a team composed of Nicholas Gillett, Edward Dommen, Jean-Pierre Gontard, Daniel Fino and Fernand Vincent. All those involved have been happy to contribute a considerable amount of time and effort to this work at no cost to the project. The production has been made possible by a generous grant from the State of Geneva, through the Féderation Genevoise de Co-operation to the Geneva Meeting of the Society of Friends.

PART I

Starting and carrying on the project

CHAPTER 1
Starting the project

A. INTRODUCTION

You are a group or an association. You have a good idea. If it is carried out, the conditions of life in your neighbourhood will become better. By answering the questions which follow, you will learn whether you can bring together all that is needed to make your idea happen and your project succeed. After you have considered all the questions you should have discovered whether you will be able to succeed by relying on your own resources alone. If that is possible, you will be masters of your own affairs.

It may be, however, that having read the questions, you will see that help from one or more partners abroad will be needed. In this case, once you have prepared your project, you should find the second part of the handbook useful.

It is important for your group to reply frankly to all the questions. If your replies are convincing not only to yourselves but to others as well, your project has a good chance of success.

B. THE AIM OF THE PROJECT

1. What is your main idea? What problem do you want to solve?
   Having made your survey or study of the possibilities in your district, have you made sure that this is the best idea among several and have you asked the advice of the right advisers?

2. Who will gain from the project?

3. How many people or families (men, women and children) will gain from the project?

4. In what ways will they gain?

5. How do you know that these people will take an interest in the project?

6. What do you plan to do so that people who are against the project do not stop its progress?

C. SETTING UP THE ORGANIZATION

In looking at the following questions, remember that it is best when the people who are likely to gain from the project take part in making plans and organizing it.

1. What body supports the project? Is it, for example, a town council, a church parish, a co-operative or some other association of people?

2. Who belongs to this body and how are they chosen?

3. Are any of them paid by the body itself? Could that fact influence their opinions about the project?

4. Who takes the main responsibility for supporting the project?

5. In case of absence, who takes their place?

6. Would you gain from links with official services or programmes? Which ones? How would you make them?

7. Would you gain from links with other organizations, national or international? Which ones? How would you make them? Are there rules in your country about receiving funds from other countries?

8. Would you gain if you were recognized or accepted by an official programme or another organization?

D. PEOPLE WORKING IN THE PROJECT

See Figure 1, which is an example of how to think about what sort of people you will need to run the project.

Note that:

-- An 'expatriate' is a person coming from abroad.

-- Each pair of figures in the table must add up to the total at the bottom. For example, 7 temporary teachers are made up of 3 volunteers and 4 paid.

-- The figures in brackets give the kind of workers still to be found. For example, the three teachers to be found will be paid, local people.

1. Where and how do you plan to recruit qualified or specialized workers?

2. Will the workers be chosen from among those who are likely to gain from the project? This is an aim worth following as much as possible.

Figure 1 People needed for the ABC training project

	Teaching long-term community development	Temporary teaching in seminars or workshops at the site of the project
Already appointed	3	4
To be found	0	3
Volunteers	0	3
Paid workers	3	1 (3 to be found)
Locally recruited	2	4 (3 to be found)
Expatriates	1	0
Committee members	1	1
Total	3	7

E. TRAINING

1. What training has already been done, or is going on now, which could meet the the needs of the project?

2. Will extra training be needed to run the project properly?

3. What kind of people will it be necessary to train? Use the categories in Figure 1 when you consider this question.

4. What technical level will they have to reach? (For example, for growing vegetables, for repairing a pump, or for becoming a builder.)

5. How many people will need to be trained?

6. Is this training to be obtained in your district or province? If not, how is it to be got?

7. Show on the timetable the training to be received (see below, Section F).

F. THE TIMETABLE

A timetable with bars provides a simple way of showing the working out of the project. This helps to make sure that everything will be done and ready at the right moment. Mark on the timetable the seasons or other factors if they affect the work and keep in mind these considerations when making a timetable for carrying out the work. Figure 2 is an example of a timetable drawn as a 'bar chart'. It uses bars or lines to show when something will be done and how long it will take to do.

Figure 2 Example of a project timetable

	Already done			Still to do										
	Nov	Dec	Jan	Feb	Mar	Apr	May	Jun	Jul	Aug	Sep	Oct	Nov	Dec
Three permanent community workers A														
Holidays for 3 permanent community workers B														
C														
Appointment of temporary teachers														
Three seminars														
Temporary teachers at work														
Visits to the place where seminars will be held														
Preparation and ordering of the teaching materials														
Publicity and booking of places														
Buying a tape recorder					X									
Ordering tables						X								
Receiving tables						X X								
Ordering chairs														
Receiving chairs								X						
Reminders: rainy season														
harvest														
sowing or planting														

COMMENTS

G. SUPPLIES NEEDED

1. Timetable for the arrival of supplies

a) Show in the timetable (Figure 2) the dates on which the various supplies will have to be ready. Then show in the timetable when you will have to start to make them, or buy them, or order them.

b) Where are you going to store the supplies when they are delivered?

c) Is there any risk that some supplies will not be to hand when they are wanted?

d) Which ones are these?

e) What do you plan to do in the case of a delay or lack of supplies?

2. Show in tables like the ones below the various materials needed for the project (machines, tools, other equipment, raw materials).

Note what supplies you already have to hand and in the last column of Figures 3 and 4, how you plan to get the rest. There are several possibilities:

Figure 3 Supplies needed once and for all

Description	Already to hand	Others to be obtained	Source of supply
Tape recorder	0	1	At Kassim's in the capital
Tables	2	3	Henry's, the carpenter, at ...
Chairs	10	30	- borrow 20 of them from the parish for evening meetings - buy 10 from Henry's

Figure 4 Supplies needed regularly

Description	To hand	Rate of use	When?	To buy How many?	Where?
Note pads	30	2 per week in the office 27 in each seminar	1 week before each seminar:* March June November	 40 45 45	Methodist Bookshop

*see Figure 2

3. Source of supply

For the last column in Figures 3 and 4 there are several possibilities:

a) Can you produce the supplies locally without having to pay money for them?

b) Can those who are going to gain from the project or their friends lend any equipment, etc. needed for short periods?

c) Can you buy the furniture or supplies from local traders? If yes, where can they be found?

d) Is it necessary to buy directly from abroad?

e) Are there any other ways of getting supplies?

H. MONEY NEEDED

1. A table of figures showing the income and expenses which are forecast for a fixed period such as a year is called a 'budget'.

    a) 'Income' or 'receipts' means the money received or paid into the account of the project.
    b) 'Expenses' means payments out of the account.

2. Examples of project budgets

You will find below four examples of budgets based on four different kinds of project.

(a) Example No. 1: Budget for a project about 'Training and Community Development (See the example, Figure 6, on page 12).

The expenses are in general as follows:

i) Costs of the people employed in the project: wages and insurance of the organizer, the community workers and other employees. In the example of the budget (Figure 6), wages are put together in a single line (7200) and the Social Security or insurance costs on another (1080). They are put together as much as possible, but to reach this figure it is necessary to work out the wages etc. for each person shown in Figure 1, for example:

Figure 5 Details of the costs of people working in the project

	Monthly wage	No. of months	Yearly pay	Insurance and Social Security	Total
Organizer	225.00	12	2700	405.00	3105.00
Community worker B	187.50	12	2250	337.50	2587.50
Community worker C	187.50	12	2250	337.50	2587.50
Sub-total for organisers	–	–	7200	1080.00	8280.00
Temporary Teacher D	150.00	3	450	67.50	517.50
" " E	125.00	3	375	56.25	431.25
" " F	125.00	2	250	37.50	287.50
" " G	100.00	1	100	15.00	115.00
(+ 3 volunteers)	–	–	–	–	–
Sub-total for teachers			1175	176.25	1351.25
Total			8375	1256.25	9631.25

The total and the sub-totals are entered in the annual budget, Figure 6.

ii) Costs related to the students or course members: lodging, food and travel.

iii) Teaching costs: documents, off-site visits.

iv) Rent or purchase of land or buildings (see also point 3a on page 11).

v) Rent or purchase of equipment. Think out when you will need the different items of equipment, and as a result when you should set about getting them. Use a timetable like Figure 2 to plan this.

vi) General expenses: stamps, telephone, telegrams, office supplies (make a list like Figure 4 to work out how much they will cost and when you will need the money), water, electricity, repairs and maintenance, bank charges etc.

Income may come from the following sources:

i) Contributions from participants in the course.

ii) Grants and gifts. They may be local or from abroad. Carefully distinguish:
- those already received for the year covered by the budget;
- promises;
- what remains to be found (see Figure 6).

    b) Example No. 2: Budget for a project leading to production (garden, agriculture, small business)

The costs or expenses are then as follows:

i) Costs of the people working in the project: wages and insurance for the organizer for the workers and other employees: the people needed should be shown in a table like Figure 1 (page 3), and their costs in a table like Figure 5. Follow the example from (a) i) above.

ii) Buying raw materials: cuttings, seeds, planks, iron etc. Think when you will have to order these things so as to have them when you need them. For this use a timetable like Figure 2.

iii) Rent or purchase of land or buildings (see point 3a page 11).

iv) Costs of production or use: maintenance of materials, vehicles, supplies, etc. These things have been listed in lists like Figure 3 or 4.

v) Costs of acquiring equipment, machines, debt repayments, etc. (see point 3c, page 11).

vi) Loans made to members.

vii) General expenses: stamps, telephone, office supplies (make a list like Figure 4 to work out how much they will cost and when you will need the money), water, electricity, maintenance, bank charges, etc.

The income comes from the following:

i) The sale of produce (cereals, fruit, vegetables, furniture, etc.).

ii) Loans repaid to the project.

iii) Grants and gifts. These grants may be local or from abroad. Carefully distinguish whether these are:

- those already received for the year covered by the budget;
- promises;
- what remains to be found

  (see Figure 6)

c) Example No. 3: Budget for a construction project

The expenses of such a project are as follows:

i) Costs of the people working in the project: fees, wages, social security and insurance for the architect, the works manager, the workers and other employees, food for volunteers. The people should be listed in a table like Figure 1, the costs connected with them should be listed in a table like Figure 4. (See the explanation under Example No. 1 (a) i) above.)

ii) Costs of building: cement, iron, wood, corrugated iron, windows, doors, paint, nails, etc. A table like Figure 3 lists the supplies, but don't forget to add to your budget transport costs and the cost of finding sources of supplies.

iii) Administrative costs: visits to officials, plans, building permits etc.

iv) General expenses: stamps, telephone, telegrams, office supplies (make a list like Figure 4 to work out how much they will cost and when you will need the money), water, electricity, maintenance, bank charges, etc.

Income comes in general from the following:

i) Local support in the form of money: subscription, gifts, etc. (for support in kind, see also point 3a, page 11).

ii) Grants and gifts: these may be local or from abroad.
Carefully distinguish whether these are:

- those already received for the year covered by the budget;
- promises;
- what remains to be found.

(see Figure 6)

d) Example No. 4: Budget for a social Project (dispensary, infant welfare clinic, etc.)

The costs are in general as follows:

i) Costs of the people working in the project: wages, social security and insurance for the organizer, for the employees, maintenance personnel, etc. The people should be listed in a table like Figure 1. The costs connected with them should be listed in a table like Figure 4.

ii) Buying medicines and other supplies, or equipment like beds, tables etc. Prepare a table like Figure 3. Think when you will have to order these things to have them when you need them: for this use a timetable like Figure 2.

iii) Rent or purchase of ground or buildings (see point 3a, page 11).

iv) General costs: administration, upkeep, etc.

v) Travel, food and lodging costs for workers who have to travel for their work.

Income may come from the following sources:

i) From the users or clients (subscriptions, charges for visits, payments for medicines etc.).

ii) Grants and gifts. They may be local or from abroad.
Carefully distinguish whether these are:
- those already received for the year covered by the budget,
- promises,
- what remains to be found.

(see Figure 6)

3. Rules for budgets of every kind

a) Contributions in kind (those which are not money but goods): they are not shown in the budget itself, but they reduce the payments which have to be made, so remember to note them at the end of the budget. (See the example in Figure 6.) If a building or some land has been given as a gift, this should be noted in the same place.

b) It is best to make out budgets for several years at a time allowing for the rise in prices which may be foreseen (this is called inflation).

c) It is desirable to separate expenses for building and costly equipment from running expenses. Put aside each year part of the cost of replacing the buildings and equipment so as to have enough money when the time comes to replace them when they are worn out. The money put aside can be kept in a savings account at the bank.

d) A sum to cover unforeseen events called a 'contingency fund'.

4. Example of a budget with detailed figures

Figure 6 shows a detailed budget of an imaginary training centre. Most of the things listed in the budget in Example no. 1 above were taken from this.

Figure 6 Example of a budget

Budget of the Centre ABC from 1 January to 31 December 1985

	Expenses			Income	
Wages & Social security & Insurance			Payments from Course members		2000
Three Community Workers	7200				
Social Sec. & Insur. for them	1080		Local resources - promises		2500
Four teachers	1175				
Social Sec. & Insur. for them	176.25	9631.25	Resources from abroad		
Training Expenses			– OXFAM 1984		1000
Food for 25 members for 30 days at 10 each day	7500		– OXFAM promise for 1985		10000
Lodging for 25 for 30 days at 5 each day	3750				
Travel for 25	2500		– SOS Sahel 1984		3000
3 seminars at 1000	3000	16750.00			
			– Quaker promises		15000
Teaching Expenses					
Course costs	1600				
Documents	2100		Sub-total		33500
Rent	2000	5700.00	To be found		3681.25
Administrative Expenses					
Stamps, telephone, telegrams	300				
Office supplies	1800				
Maintenance	300				
Meetings	200				
Bank charges	100				
Contingencies*	200	2900.00			
Equipment					
Brought: a tape-recorder	1000				
3 tables at 200	600				
20 chairs at 30	600	2200.00			
		37181.25			37181.25

*It is always necessary to explain afterwards what these unforeseen 'contingencies' have been.

N.B. During the courses the teachers will stay without charge with members of the committee.

CHAPTER 2
Running the project

A. INTRODUCTION

At least once a year the following questions must be asked: are the people concerned with the project satisfied with the way it is going? If they are not, should the project be altered? Should the timetable and budget be corrected? (A change in the timetable will probably mean that the budget will have to be changed.)

B. KEEPING TO THE TIMETABLE

At the time when the project was planned, you made a timetable to show what had to be done each month (see Figure 2 and Chapter 1, Section F). Make sure you are following it. If not, you will have to adjust what remains to be done.

1. Work finished

Show each month on the timetable what has actually been finished and ask these questions:

1. Are we following the timetable as planned? If so, all is well; the timetable needs no change.

2. Are we ahead of the timetable? If so, why? Can the timetable for the months to come be changed to take advantage of this? In particular have you over-estimated the time needed for parts of the work? In this case, keep it in mind when you change the timetable.

3. Have we got behind? If so, why? Can the timetable for the months to come be changed to take advantage of this? In particular have you over-estimated the time needed for parts of the work? In this case, keep it in mind when you change the timetable. If you have to change the timetable you will most likely have to change the budget as well (see paragraphs 3 and 4 in Section C below).

2. Work still to be done

Does it seem that everything is in order for the months to come so that the work can go forward as planned? For example, are the people on whom you depend likely to be available when you need them? Will the delivery dates of supplies be met or are they likely to be changed? Have all supplies listed in the budget been needed, or have they been too little or too much?

C. MONEY

It is wise to have several different people each responsible for a different aspect of money matters so that they are not all in the hands of one person. The money itself should be in the hands of someone who is trusted by all. Another person, such as a young school leaver for example, can keep the accounts.

1. The accounts

An accounting system should be set up to know whether the income is equal to the expenditure, or to know where the money has come from or gone to.

a) The accounting system

An accounting system is a set of rules for keeping track of income and expenditure.

Here is an example of a simple accounting system:
- A cash book
- A bank book
- A record of donors
- A record of 'third parties': creditors, debtors, etc.
- A working balance sheet
- A 'profit and loss' account
- A capital account, including the financial side of expensive items owned (buildings, land, vehicles, equipment, animals, etc.)

This plan can be further simplified by opening only four accounts (money in and out).
- Cash
- Bank
- Donors
- Working/'profit and loss'

The simplest accounting requires:

- Two books, one for cash and the other for the bank if you've opened an account.

- A file and something to make holes in papers: after punching holes you keep all the documents needed to support the accounts in chronological (date) order.

- A locked cash box for keeping money and the cheque book from the bank, also the receipts which have not yet been filed. (But don't delay in filing them! It is best to file them as soon as they come in.

When money is taken from the cash box or the bank and spent, there must be a paper kept to show how it was used. If that is really not possible (it seldom happens), write a note yourself, sign it and, if possible, get it signed by a witness.

b) The cash book

The cash book and the bank book are kept in the following way:

Figure 7 Cash Book of Project ABC

Date		Number of the item	Payments out	Payments in	Balance
1985					
3 July	Cash balance	1		125	125
5 July	Transfer from bank	2		1000	1125
8 July	June wages of J. Bita.	3	225		900
10 July	Stamps bought	4	20		880
15 July	Barnabe for nails	5	5		875
16 July	Petrol for transport.	6	13		862

The different tasks in keeping accounts are these:

1) Expenditure or payments out

   i) An invoice or bill is received, etc.;
   ii) A cheque is drawn, or the money is taken out;
   iii) A receipt is asked for or put ready (see model below) to be signed by the person receiving the cheque or the money;
   iv) The payment is made and the receipt is put in the file;
   v) Without delay this is written in the cash book or bank book.
   vi) A number is given to the receipt and this number is put on the line showing the payment (see Figure 7, page 15).

If someone needs to take some money, but doesn't know exactly how much he will need, he should leave a note saying how much he has taken and why, like this:

Figure 8   Receipt for an advance to a member of the project for expenses

> I have taken 150.— for travelling expenses on my trip to Bagare
> Signed: Barnabe Smith
> Witness: Joseph Ngock
> Date: 9 September 1986

This is an expenditure and should be recorded as one in the cash book. When he has made his expenditure, he should return the money left over and obtain a receipt (see below). It could look like Figure 10, or like this:

Figure 9   Receipt for unspent money returned

> Barnabe Smith has returned 12.— left over after his trip to Bagare
> Signed: Joseph Ngock
> Treasurer
> Date: 20 September 1986

2) Receipts or payments in

1) Receipts, whether received or given, are in duplicate, one copy is kept and the other goes to the person who has paid the money.

2) They are written in the cash book or bank book, where they have a number (see Figure 7).

3) The number is written on the receipt.

3) Loans

In many kinds of project money has to be lent to members. This could happen, for example, in associations of farmers or craftsmen. Members may need an advance of money to meet their expenses until they sell what they have produced. In some cases also money may be lent to employees.

Project leaders are often farmers or craftsmen themselves, and may need loans for their work like other members. It is, however, very important that project leaders should not take advantage of their position to obtain loans for purposes which are different from the purposes of the project. It would be unfair to the other members.

The project should make strict rules about:

- Who may borrow;
- For what purposes they may borrow;
- In what conditions they may borrow.

Everyone must obey the rules. If a loan is made it is necessary to have a receipt signed by the borrower and to say exactly how and when he is going to repay it. It is wise to make the loan and to have the receipt signed in the presence of a witness who should also sign the receipt.

Here is a model for a receipt for a loan:

Figure 10 Receipt

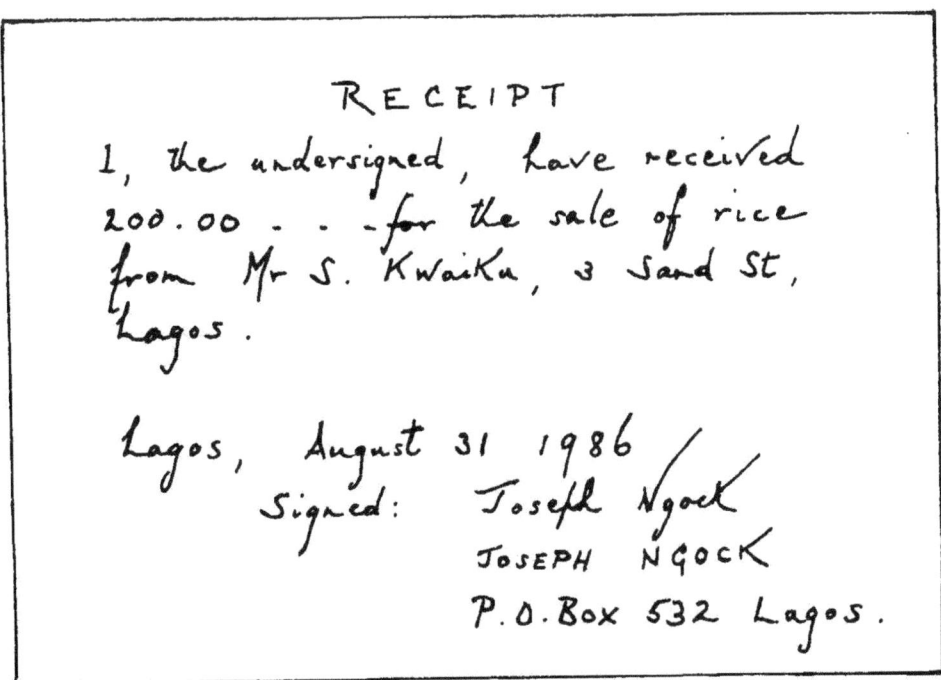

Figure 11 Receipt for a loan

Receipt

I, the undersigned, agree that I have received the sum of 200.00 from Mr. Joseph Ngock of Bamako.

I undertake to repay this sum as follows:

Date	Amount	In letters
31.07.1985	20.00	twenty
31.08.1985	50.00	fifty
30.09.1985	50.00	fifty
31.10.1985	50.00	fifty
30.11.1985	30.00	thirty

Bamako 1 July 1985   Signature ....

                                                M. Cisse
                                                P.O. Box 25 Bamako

Witness's Signature ....
                                                  Joseph Gabioli
                                                P.O. Box 325

If it is a loan with interest, write it on the receipt and work out the monthly amount which has to be added to the monthly repayments of capital. (See example Figure 12, page 19.) Some lenders give out cards showing figures like those in this receipt above. When a repayment is made it is marked on the card.

Figure 12 Loan agreement

<u>Loan agreement</u>

I, the undersigned, acknowledge the receipt of the sum of 2100, from AB co-operative, 3 Freeman Street, Lomé.

Interest: 8% a year

Repayment: in three years; 700 at the end of each year starting 30 June 1987.

Lomé, 1 July 1986   Signature ....
                                      Barnabe Wilson
                                      P.O. Box 139 Lomé

                    Witness's Signature ....
                                      L. Bita

<u>Annual repayments over three years</u>

1 July 1986	Loan	2100	
30 June 1987	Repayment of Capital		700
	Interest 8% on 2100		168
			868
30 June 1988	Repayment of Capital		700
	Interest 8% on 1400		112
			812
30 June 1989	Repayment of Capital		700
	Interest 8% on 700		56
			756

---

2. Making monthly budgets

A budget has no doubt been worked out at the outset for a period of a year at a time. But a whole year is too long a period for keeping proper track of the money side of a project. For the current year the budget must be divided up into months to compare with the timetable.

Making a yearly budget like Figure 6 for the following year can be done in one go, for example in the month of November. We here explain the monthly budget for the current year.

To keep a better control over your monthly expenses and to make sure that the project is progressing as planned, it is helpful to draw up a set of monthly budgets like Figure 13. One way of preparing the budget for the year is to work out the expenses for each month as in Figure 13, and then add up each item (row) for every month to get the yearly total.

3. Needs for money in the course of the year

It is always necessary to have money in cash or at the bank to meet your expenses when they occur.

For that you need to forecast:

1st The expenses each month and/or for a period of two or three months (see Sub-section 2 above).

2nd The time to ask for the money needed for expenses (by month or by period.)

If the project is receiving outside assistance and your partner sends money twice a year on 15 December and 15 May, ask him to send the amount you need to cover your expenses in the period between the two payments. The example below, Figure 13, can be useful for this kind of forecast.

Figure 13
Table C. 3A
Monthly budget of a training centre
Budget of the Lomé Centre 1984

Imaginary currency and amounts

EXPENDITURE	Jan	Feb	Mar	Apr	May	Jun	Jul	Aug	Sept	Oct	Nov	Dec	Total
Wages, insurance	690	690	1027	802	690	915	915	690	690	822	1027	691	9649
Food	625	625	625	625	625	625	625	625	625	625	625	625	7500
Lodging	310	310	310	310	325	310	310	310	310	310	310	325	3750
Travel	500	-	-	500	-	300	500	-	200	-	200	300	2500
Seminars	100	400	500	-	100	400	500	-	100	400	500	-	3000
Course costs & meeting place	-	300	-	200	-	200	300	-	400	-	200	-	1600
Teaching documents	500	200	100	300	200	300	100	100	100	-	100	100	2100
Rent	-	-	500	-	-	500	-	-	500	-	-	500	2000
Stamps and Telephone	100	-	-	50	-	-	-	100	-	-	50	-	300
Office supplies	150	150	150	150	150	150	150	150	150	150	150	150	1800
Maintenance	-	100	-	-	50	-	50	-	50	-	50	-	300
Meetings	-	-	50	-	-	50	-	100	-	-	-	-	200
Bank charges	-	-	-	-	-	-	40	-	-	-	40	20	100
Extras	-	-	50	-	-	50	-	-	50	-	-	50	200
Tape recorder				1000									1000
Tables					600								600
Chairs						600							600
Monthly total	2975	2775	3312	3937	2740	4400	3490	2075	3175	2307	3252	2761	37199
Cumulative total	2975	5750	9062	12999	15739	20139	23629	25704	28879	31186	34438	37199	

Budget prepared 10 November 1984 by ....

Figure 13 (Continued)
Table C. 3B
Budget of a training centre
Monthly budget of the ABC Centre at Lomé

INCOME

Receipts of which the dates are known	Carried Forward	Jan	Feb	Mar	Apr	May	June	July	Aug	Sept	Oct	Nov	Dec	To be Fixed	Total
Fees from the course members		250	150	150	150	150	150	250	150	150	150	150	150		2000
Local Support				1000						1500					2500
OXFAM	1000					10000									11000
SOS Sahel	3000														3000
Monthly total	4000	250	150	1150	150	10150	150	250	150	1650	150	150	150		18500
Cumulative monthly total	4000	4250	4400	5550	5700	15850	16000	16250	16400	18050	18200	18350	18500		

Income at dates still to be fixed															
Ministry of Education grant														15000	15000

Figure 14 Comparison of income and expenses

1984

Month	Cumulative amount of monthly expenditure	Cumulative amount of expected income
Carried forward	–	4000
Jan	2975	4250
Feb	5750	4400
Mar	9062	5550
Apr	12999	5700
May	15739	15850
June	20139	16000
July	23629	16250
Aug	25704	16400
Sept	28879	18050
Oct	31186	18200
Nov	34438	18350
Dec	37199	18500

Note: The cumulative amount of monthly expenses is the same as the bottom line of example Figure 13 (expenditure). The cumulative amount of expected income is the same as the line 'cumulative monthly total' of Figure 13 (income).

In the example above, Figure 14, you will see that with the timetable of expected income and expenditure the project will already be out of money in February (cumulative expenditure 5750, cumulative income only 4400). The OXFAM grant expected in May will prevent a deficit only in that month. In June, expenditure will have reached 20139, while income will only have been 16000.

To avoid these difficulties it may be necessary for example
- to ask OXFAM to pay earlier in the year.
- to ask the Ministry of Education who have not said when they would pay, to send half their grant in January and the rest in June at the latest.

4. Control of the budget

a) Control of the monthly budget

To know if your monthly expenses are what you expected, check them each month. The following table may be useful as an example.

Figure 15 Control of the monthly budget

January 1985

	The month's expenditure shown in the budget	The month's actual expenditure	Difference
Wages and insurance	690	670	-20
Food	625	635	+10
Lodging	310	310	-
Travel	500	600	+100
Seminars	100		-100
Course costs	-	-	-
Teaching documents	500	400	-100
Rent	-	-	-
Stamps & telephone	100	280	+180
Office supplies	150	110	-40
Meetings	-	-	-
Bank charges			
Extras or contingencies (water brought by truck due to a pump failure)*		50	+50
Tape recorder	-	-	-
Tables	-	-	-
Chairs	-	-	-
	2975	3055	+80

* The item 'extra' is not a way to cover up. It is essential to explain afterwards what the expenditure actually was.

Any difference between the budget and actual expenditure must be explained, so that you can decide whether you should increase your budget for the rest of the year or change the project (including the timetable like Figure 2) so that expenditure remains within what the project can afford. In this example 80 more than the amount shown in the budget has been spent.

You should do the same with income. Compare the expenditure and income each month. How do they balance?

1) If income and expenditure balance, that is fine so long as you have kept to the timetable. If not, go over the timetable again for the coming months. If you are following the timetable make sure that prices have not changed from those used in the budget for whatever you are going to have to buy (inflation). Make sure also that income will keep coming in as planned. If necessary think again about the monthly budgets for the next period.

2) If they do not balance:

   i) Have you spent more or less than you planned? Why? Is it because you are ahead of your timetable? If yes, look again at the budget and timetable or even the programme of work. You might in the end be able to add to your activities.

   ii) Is it because prices have gone up? Look at your budget for the next months if you have to buy the same things in the future. In any case it will be necessary either to spend less or to increase the income in order to balance the budget. What are you going to do? It may be necessary to change the timetable or even your aims.

   iii) Is it because the income is less than planned? Are there delays in the payments? Why? Will it be enough to send a reminder to those who are late in paying? If not, what are the causes of the delay? Will they be overcome in the near future? If not, you will have to cut the income side of your budget, and the expenditure side so that the new budget still balances. It may be necessary to change the timetable or the programme as a result. Have you fewer dues-paying members than you planned? Should you change the level of the dues? Have you fixed the prices at which you provide goods or services too high or too low?

Should you, therefore, change your prices? Or advertise your goods better? Or should you change your policies in other ways? In every case of this kind you will have to change the timetable or the budget.

b) Control by the yearly budget

Ask yourself the same questions as those in sub-section 4 (a) for the yearly budget, but only once a year in, say, November.

c) Control by the monthly cumulative totals

If, from February onwards, a total is made for the expenses and income since the beginning of the year it is possible to compare the actual results with the budget figures even more easily. In this case the table looks like this:

Figure 16 Cumulative expenditure and income month by month

Expenses	Budget from 1.1.84 to 31.5.1984	Expenditure from 1.1.84 to 31.5.1984	Difference
Wages and insurance	3899	4020	+ 121
Food	3125	3050	− 75

etc. (follow the details in Figure 13)

5. The yearly accounts

a) The accounts

At the end of the year the accounts for the past year must be made out. You have written out a budget according to the model in Figure 6. During the year you have written down the actual expenses and income under the same headings as are to be found in the budget. This compares what you planned with what really did happen (see Figure 16). Since this has been done the accounts are not difficult to finish: all that remains to be done is to take the cumulative totals for the twelve months of the year for each item of expenditure and add them up, as in the last column of Figure 13 (expenditure).

b) Auditing the accounts

To avoid mistakes it is always better to have one's work checked.
Auditing the accounts is a check to keep the confidence of:

- the members of the organization and those who are going to gain from the project. (An explanation with the use of a blackboard helps many people to understand how accounts are done.)

- the donors of money, both local and elsewhere.

So it is necessary to choose as auditors one or two people who have the confidence of those who need to be reassured. The auditors must therefore not be committee members; they must be wholly independent of the committee. In some countries they must be professional auditors.

In some projects the accounting is simple, and ordinary members of the organization, or those who are to gain, may be asked. A person outside the project may be asked, one who is widely trusted such as a teacher or priest. If the accounts are more complicated it is better to ask a professional accountant (include his fee in the budget!).

Some partners abroad ask for special ways of auditing accounts. If you want money from them, you must find out what they want <u>before</u> starting to keep accounts, so that you can agree on a way of accounting which meets their wishes (see Chapter 3 in the second part of the handbook, B.5).

If the partner abroad asks for accounts which are more complicated than are needed to run the project properly (in other words more complicated than the models of Chapter 1 of the first part (section H), or if he insists on expensive auditors, it is fair to ask him to pay the cost of what he is asking for.

c) Working with the auditors:

The yearly accounts are given to the auditors, with the cash book and all supporting papers. The auditors should be given the bank statements, including the balance for the end of the year, and the cheque book with its stubs. They will want to count the cash in the cash-box.

The auditors may have comments to make about how the accounts have been kept. They should always be asked for a written report, which must be made public. This will help you to keep better accounts in years to come.

D. THE MANAGEMENT OF SUPPLIES

If the project has goods or produce to store for some time, a record should be kept for each type.

Example: Sacks of millet in the cereal bank of Quahigouya

Figure 17 Record of millet stocks

Date	Description	IN	OUT	STOCK
1 July	Brought in by X	3		3
1 July	Brought in by Y	5		8
1 July	Brought in by Z	1		9
2 July	Taken out by A		1	8
3 July	Taken out by B		1	7
	Eaten by rats		1	6

This table may also be used for supplies needed for carrying out the project and which are valuable or which may be difficult to replace quickly. These supplies may be for building the project (nails, iron, sacks of cement, etc.), or used in operating it (petrol, stationery, medicines, etc.). Remember to write down in the record what is broken, lost or damaged.

For each kind of goods a record like the one above is needed. These records will help you: (a) to make sure that nothing is being stolen; (b) to know in good time when to order more.

Don't wait until the stock is finished before ordering more! For example, if it takes a week to get supplies and the project uses two each week, you must order again when the stock is down to three. When the stock drops to this figure, action must be taken to order more. The figure must be shown at the head of each stock record as a guide to whoever looks after the stores.

E. MANAGING THE PEOPLE WORKING IN THE PROJECT

Are the people on whom you depend working as expected?
Are the volunteers and wage-earners as many and as hard-working as you planned?

Or are they more numerous and hard-working? Congratulations! Why not take advantage of their enthusiasm to speed up or enlarge the project? In this case you should review the timetable, the budget or the programme.

Or are they fewer than expected, or are they not working as effectively as hoped? Why? Are they losing interest in their work? Should you alter the project after discussing it with them? Does the timetable not fit the times when they are free? Will there be more people free at another time of year? In this case change the timetable. Or is the shortage of people likely to go on? In this case you may have to spread the project over a longer period or change the method of work. That would lead most likely to a change of the timetable and of the budget or even of the aims of the project.

If you have wage-earners is all going well with them? Are they fewer or less hard-working than planned? If so, are their wages the same as for others in the region? Should they be changed? If so, the budget will also have to be changed.

Do you have the skilled or technical manpower you need? If not, are you offering them pay at the normal level for your region? Should you offer more (which will mean changing the budget)?

If particular skills are simply not available, can you change the way of working so as to be less dependent on them? Should one of your number be trained in this skill? If so, put this training into your programme of work and alter the budget and timetable to cover it.

Are the organizers (treasurer, secretary, foreman, etc.) still doing what is expected of them? If not, what are you going to do?

It is natural that from time to time one of the organizers may wish to leave his job. It is important to foresee such changes so as to be able to find a new person before he leaves. Encourage your team to say far enough ahead if they are planning to leave so that you can get people in time to take their places.

It sometimes happens that the project has to dismiss one of the team. Should you have to do this, respect the provisions of the labour law and in particular make the payments to him which the law requires.

F. RELATIONSHIPS WITH PARTNERS

Are you satisfied with the links between your project and official bodies? If not, should the way the project is being carried out, or its aims, be changed?

Are you satisfied with your partners? In particular do their payments come at the right time and in the amount expected? If not, should the timetable or the monthly or yearly budget be changed? Would it be useful to change the aims of the project to suit the aims of the partner?

Have you kept your partner well informed about how the project is going?

PART II

Working with your partners

INTRODUCTION

The success of a project depends on its leaders, but it will only succeed if it attracts the active support of those who are supposed to benefit from it and if it has been well thought out both in its practical results and in the way it is to be carried out. The first part of this handbook is planned to help people involved in a project to think systematically about how to design and run it.

If they can plan it and carry it out by relying only on their own resources, they have the best chance of keeping their independence - carrying out the project as they wish and meeting their needs as they themselves see them.

Nevertheless it is sometimes necessary to get outside support, either technical help or funds or goods to carry out a useful well-planned project. Then the support of a partner must be sought. The outside partner will want to know three things before he agrees to help:

1) Does the project fit in with his own aims? It is obvious, for example, that an organization specializing in supporting education will not be interested in a project for building wells.

2) Is the project properly planned?

3) Does it have the interest and active support of those concerned, (without which the project cannot succeed)?

The people involved in the project are doubtless more interested in carrying out their project than in filling up forms to satisfy a possible partner. Similarly the partner can read report after report without ever understanding what is really going on in the project. In the end this knowledge can only come with mutual confidence based on good relationships built over a long period. As a Swedish donor said:

> 'If broad agreement on objectives exists, aid funds can be freely disbursed for purposes specified by the recipient and also shifted between projects in accordance with the circumstances. It is in this context that one should see the importance attached to the choice of recipient and to relations of mutual confidence.

The second part of this handbook tries to keep the questions put by the partner to the project organizers to as few as possible. This means limiting them to those which have to be put to know what kind of project it is, to be sure that it has been well planned, and lastly to meet the needs of good management (especially financial management).

It must be remembered that the external partner also depends on the support of his members, who provide the funds for the projects in which he shares. These members wish to be kept informed of what is done with their money, so that they feel involved. For that, direct contact is best but when that is not possible the project organizer should give a little time to describing at regular intervals what is going on in the project. This kind of report will be more vivid if it follows no model laid down in advance.

CHAPTER 1
The partner abroad explains who he is

It is simplest for the partner abroad to explain who he is, to say what kind of work he likes to support and to state his own aims. The project organizer can then decide more easily if his own project corresponds to the partner's interests.

This page can be completed by the organizations which distribute this handbook, that is to say by the donor partner. It can include:

(a) The names of the organizers of the partner organization and their address:

....

(b) The principles on which the organization works and the criteria for project selection can be put in here.

....
....
....
....
....
....

This is who we are. Does your project fit our aims?

....
....
....
....
....

CHAPTER 2

The project organizer puts his project to his partner

Give the partner the information asked for under the headings below with as much detail as possible.

1. Name of the project, including its official name if different from its usual one.

2. Name of the organizer responsible for the project.

3. Postal address

4. How can the organizer be contacted urgently? (telephone, telex, etc.): give the number and any other information which will help to reach him.

5. What are the best ways of transferring funds?
    - bank: the number of the bank account.
      name and address of the bank.
    - post office: the post office's name and address.
    - other ways: (explain)

So that we can get to know you better we would like you to give us a fairly short account of

    (a) who you are (b) your history as a group (c) your problems
    (d) your ideas about what needs doing and (e) your plan of action.

Write your replies freely but briefly.

We would like you now to answer the following questions in more detail. This information is needed so that your partner can better judge how to help your project effectively.

A. THE NATURE OF THE PROJECT

1. What is the aim of the project? Why was it chosen?

2. Who will gain from the project? Have they worked together before?

3. How many people or families (men, women and children) will gain from the project? (A rough number is good enough.)

4. In what way will they gain?

B. THE STRUCTURE AND ORGANIZATION OF THE PROJECT

1. What is the body which supports the project? (Is it, for example, a town council, a parish, a co-operative or other group?)

2. How is this body made up and how are its members chosen?

3. Do you object to your partner writing to this body for a reference?

4. Among these members are there any people being paid by the body itself?

5. Who are its organizers?

    To answer question 5 follow the model below:
    Name:
    His job within the body:
    Other jobs: .....
    (employment, political activity, leadership in other groups)

6. Is your group recognized by any official government service or department? Which ones?

7. Is your group a part of any nation-wide or international organization? Which one?

C. PEOPLE WORKING IN THE PROJECT

Put in here a table like Figure 1 (page 3).

D. THE TIMETABLE OF THE PROJECT

Put in here a bar chart like Figure 2 (page 5).

E. SUPPLIES AND EQUIPMENT

Put in here tables like Figures 3 and 4 (page 6).

F. TRAINING

1. Will people need to be trained if the project is to succeed?

2. What kind of training will they need?

3. What level of skill should they reach? (For example, in vegetable growing, pump maintenance, building work or teacher training).

4. How many will need training?

5. Is this training already to be had in your area? If not how can it be obtained?

6. Show on the timetable (which may cover more than one year) all the training which will be given.

CHAPTER 3
Dialogue between partners

A. INTRODUCTION

Good relations depend on good understanding. To avoid surprises and misunderstanding the two partners should exchange information and views freely.

These exchanges have a formal or official part to meet specific requirements (audited annual accounts, a report to the partner's annual general meeting), but they also have a more informal part based on a frequent exchange of letters and visits if possible. This is every bit as important as the formal part.

B. THE DUTIES OF THE PARTNER ABROAD

1. The partner abroad must state clearly who he is and what his aims are so that the project organizers can decide whether it would be useful to approach him in the first place. (see Chapter 1 of the second part).

2. The partner abroad who expects to get a request for renewed support every year must say well in advance by what date this request must be received (see also No. 2 in Section C below).

3. If the partner abroad is not planning to go on supporting a project for a long time - for example, if his aim is that a project should be able to stand on its own feet after a certain number of years - the project organizers must be told well in advance, and at least one whole year before the end of the partnership.

4. If the partner abroad wishes to get regular reports of activities, the dates and forms of report must be clearly stated in advance (see Section C below).

5. Financial reports will doubtless be required, at least once a year. The partner abroad must explain in advance how he needs these drawn up and audited.

C. DUTIES OF THE PROJECT ORGANIZERS

1. The organizers must send the partner abroad a regular report on the activities of the project. The best would be to send the timetable (Figure 2) and show what changes have been made since the last report. A page or two may be added to explain changes in aims, unforeseen difficulties or simply how the project has been going.

2. The organizers must send regularly - normally once a year - to the partner abroad a request to renew the support which he is receiving, if the relationship is to continue. The partner abroad will have stated clearly the date by which this must be done (see No. 2 in Section B above), but the organizer needs to be sure to post the request perhaps several weeks earlier, as the post is often slow.

3. The organizer has also to send accounts (see Figure 6 and pages 14-28)

4. Each time the partner abroad makes a payment to the project, the organizers should write at once to say it has come and state the amount received in local money. This prevents later misunderstandings, since the partner abroad does not necessarily know the current exchange rate or bank charges or the various payments which have to be made along the way.

5. It is necessary to make official reports. These are essential for a good working relationship between the partners. In addition it is good to keep the partner informed about what is going on and the hopes and difficulties of those who are carrying out the project. More personal letters and photographs can help the partners to know and understand each other better.

D. VISITS TO THE PROJECT

1. It can be very useful for the partner to make a personal visit so as to get to know what is going on in the project. Visitors may have good advice to give even if they find it difficult to understand all the details of surroundings strange to them. Moreover they may well learn things useful for meeting needs which are felt in the developed countries of the North. Put yourself in the shoes of your visitors, if you can.

2. When the project gets visitors from the North the organizers should watch the following points:

   a) The members of the project should not suffer on account of their tradition of generous hospitality.

   b) If the organizers write well in advance, the visitors may be asked to bring something which is hard to get locally, such as spare parts.

   c) It is good to take advantage of such a visit by telling the visitors about the achievements, the spirit and cultural values of the project and the region.

   d) Can the visitor take something home with him which will make it easier for him to show his organization what the project is about?

If you like, start keeping your records by copying the sheets on the following three pages into your own accounts book.

Monthly Budget Control Sheet

Month .... Year .....

	The month's expenditure shown in the budget	The month's actual expenditure	Difference
Wages and insurance			
Food			
Lodging			
Travel			
Seminars			
Course costs			
Teaching documents			
Rent			
Stamps & telephone			
Office supplies			
Meetings			
Bank charges			
Extras or contingencies (water brought by truck due to a pump failure)			
Tape recorder			
Tables			
Chairs			
TOTAL			

Cash Book

Date	Item	Number of the item	Payments out	Payments in	Balance

Receipt for a loan

Receipt

I, the undersigned, agree that I have received the sum of
from

I undertake to repay this sum as follows:

Date   Amount   In letters

                              Signature ....

                        Witness's Signature ....

www.ingramcontent.com/pod-product-compliance
Ingram Content Group UK Ltd.
Pitfield, Milton Keynes, MK11 3LW, UK
UKHW050227150426
5217IPUK00024B/1678